BUILDINGS AT WORK

Sports Stadiums

ELIZABETH ENCARNACION

QED Publishing

Copyright © QED Publishing 2007

First published in the UK in 2007 by
QED Publishing
A Quarto Group company
226 City Road
London EC1V 2TT
www.qed-publishing.co.uk

A catalogue record for this book is available from the British Library.

ISBN 978 1 84538 673 3

Written by Elizabeth Encarnacion
Designed by Rahul Dhiman (Q2A Media)
Series Editor Honor Head
Foldout illustration by Ian Naylor
Picture Researcher Sujatha Menon

Publisher Steve Evans
Creative Director Zeta Davies
Senior Editor Hannah Ray

Printed and bound in China

Picture credits
Key: T = top, B = bottom, C = centre, L = left, R = right, FC = front cover

Luke Daniek/ **Istockphoto**: 4-5 (background), Ryan Riley: 5t,
London Aerial Photo Library / Alamy: 5m, 6-7 (background), Greg Valiquette: 7t,
Steve Rossen: 7m, **Sydney Photography Service/ Photolibrary**: 8-9 (background), MiRea: 9t,
REUTERS/ Kai Pfaffenbach: 9b, Richard Gross/ **Corbis**: 10-11 (background) Carrie Martz: 11t,
Danny Lehman/ **Corbis**: 11b, Arcaid/ **Alamy**: 12b, **EuroStyle Graphics, photographersdirect.com**: 13,
Mr Sloth: 14-15 (background), **POPPERFOTO**/**Alamy**: 15t, Hoberman Collection/ **Corbis**: 15b,
Ales Fevzer/ **Corbis**: 16-17 (background), Bryan Allison: 17t, Yann Arthus-Bertrand/ **Corbis**: 22-23 (background),
Michael Kim/ **Corbis**: 23b, Mark Read/ **NASCAR**: 25b, **PICHON/ CORBIS SYGMA**: 26-27 (background),
Tim de Waele/ **Corbis**: 27b, **Photo Researchers, Inc./ Photolibrary**: 28-29 (background),
Lucian Coman/ **Shutterstock**: 29t, Gerald French/ **Corbis**: 30-31 (background), Jose Fuste Raga/
Corbis: 31t, Joey Bordelon/Icon SMI/ **Corbis**: 31b, **REUTERS**/ POOL New: 33t.

Words in **bold** can be found in the Glossary on page 34.

CONTENTS

SPORTS STADIUMS

People have gathered in **stadiums** to watch sporting events for thousands of years. The earliest stadium we know about was the original Olympic Stadium in Olympia, in Ancient Greece. However, the most famous ancient stadium is the Colosseum in Rome, Italy. Two thousand years ago, gladiator battles and other public events took place in this amazing building. Early stadiums, such as the Olympic Stadium and the Colosseum, had the same basic parts as modern stadiums: a central area for playing a sport and viewing stands for **spectators**. Modern stadium builders have made sporting events even more fun to visit by adding comfortable seats, food and souvenir shops and giant television screens.

FACT!

The playing surface at Velky Strahovsky Stadion in Prague, Czech Republic, is so huge that nine football pitches could fit onto it!

INDOOR SPORTS

Sports such as basketball or ice hockey are usually played indoors, in buildings called arenas. These indoor arenas have permanent roofs and are shaped like a circle. Outdoor stadiums are often shaped more like an oval.

◄ This is the American Airlines Arena which is the home of the Miami Heat basketball team, in the United States.

▼ The Colosseum in Rome was built nearly 2000 years ago and is one of the first ever stadiums.

Cover it up!

Most modern stadiums are built with some kind of roof to cover the seats. But not all roofs are the same. A roof with a hole in the middle above the playing area allows natural grass to grow on the ground below. A **retractable roof** can be opened on days when the weather is good and closed when the weather is bad.

▲ Many outdoor stadiums have roofs that cover the people who are watching the match, but not the grass pitch.

FOOTBALL STADIUMS

A typical football stadium has a rectangular playing field, surrounded by **tiers** of seats. Service areas such as food stands, souvenir shops and toilets may be placed behind the seats, on the outer edge of the stadium. Most football stadiums are only partly, or temporarily, covered by a roof because they have natural grass that needs light to grow. Other stadiums are completely indoors and use **artificial turf**.

FACT!

The Maracanã Stadium in Brazil hosted the largest crowd ever to attend a football match during the 1950 World Cup final. More than 200 000 fans were in the stands!

IT'S ELECTRIC!

Many stadiums now have giant, high-definition video boards to show scores, instant replays and game highlights to the spectators. These super-sized television screens give every fan a close-up look at the match. Cameras located around the stadium send pictures to a control room, where editors decide which images to put on the big screen.

▲ The Miami Dolphins are an American Football team. The high-definition video screens at the Dolphins Stadium in Miami, USA, are some of the largest in the world.

▼ Members of the grounds staff check the health of the grass pitch every day.

▲ Old Trafford Stadium is home to Manchester United football team. It can hold more than 76 000 fans.

Terrific turf

Where there is natural grass, the **grounds staff** works very hard to keep the playing field in good condition. They **fertilize** the grass and use a sprinkler system to make sure it is watered regularly. The field also needs a good **drainage system**, so that water doesn't collect into puddles. Many stadiums even have heating systems under the pitch to keep the grass warm during very cold weather. The grounds staff will cut the grass about three times a week during the peak growing season.

athletics competitions, which include both track and **field events**, take place on a grass pitch about the size of a football field, surrounded by an oval-shaped running track. The track is usually six to ten **lanes** wide, and to do one lap, each athlete runs 400 metres. The surface of the track is designed to conserve the runners' energy and give them more **traction**. Two kinds of rubber are used to make the surface, which absorbs the force of the runners' feet and bounces this energy back to them. Track events include **sprinting**, long-distance races, **hurdles** and **relay races**.

▼ This Olympic Stadium in Sydney, Australia, is used for both athletics events and football games.

FACT!

The Stade de France in Paris has **retractable seats** that cover the athletics track during football games so that fans can sit closer to the action.

Jumping

Jumping events are held on the **infield**. Athletes doing long jump and triple jump use a straight take-off track that is similar to the running track. The athlete then leaps into a sand-filled pit. The high jump and pole vault events both use a horizontal bar held up by two upright poles. The pole vault bar is much higher than the high jump bar. A thick, padded mat protects the athletes when they land after these jumps.

After each long jump or triple jump, the sand is smoothed out again. ▶

THROWING

The infield is also used for the throwing events. In the javelin event, athletes run down a short track, then throw the javelin as far as they can into the field. Competitors in the shot put, hammer and discus events stand in a small, circle-shaped area. They spin around very quickly to gain force and when they reach the edge of the circle they fling their object across the field, where the distance of the throw is measured.

◀ A net around the throwing circle protects other athletes and spectators from the heavy hammer.

BALLPARKS

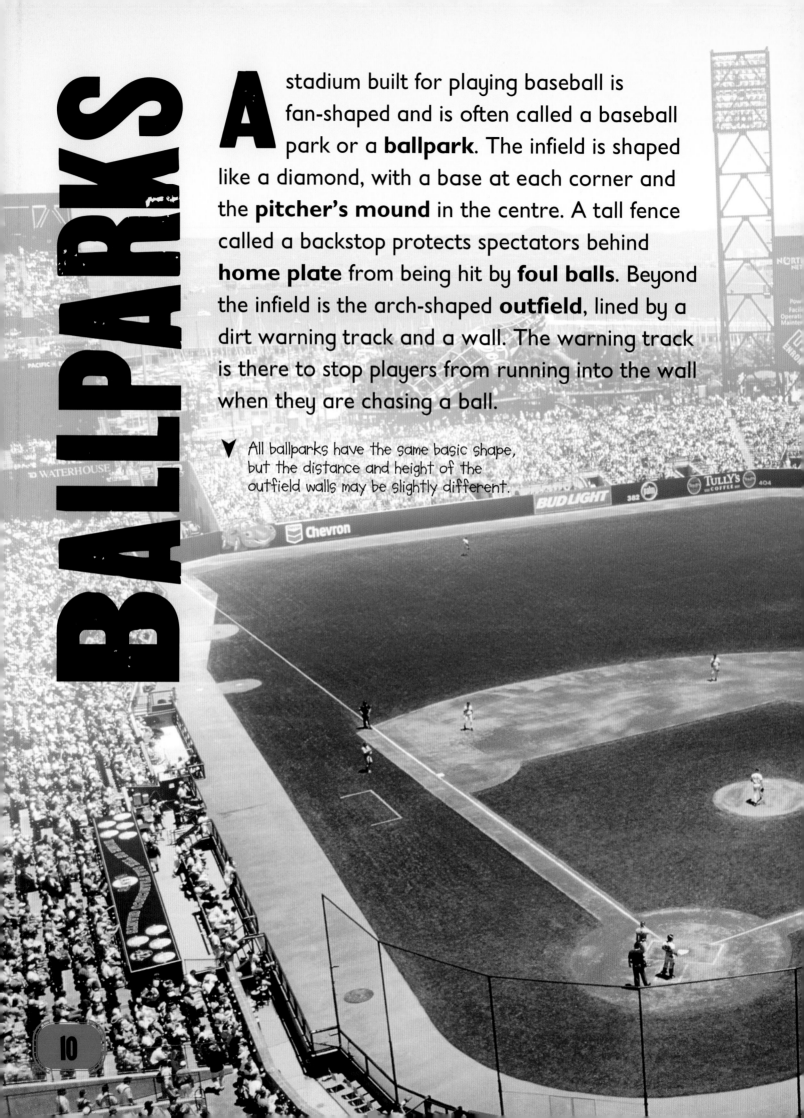

A stadium built for playing baseball is fan-shaped and is often called a baseball park or a **ballpark**. The infield is shaped like a diamond, with a base at each corner and the **pitcher's mound** in the centre. A tall fence called a backstop protects spectators behind **home plate** from being hit by **foul balls**. Beyond the infield is the arch-shaped **outfield**, lined by a dirt warning track and a wall. The warning track is there to stop players from running into the wall when they are chasing a ball.

▼ All ballparks have the same basic shape, but the distance and height of the outfield walls may be slightly different.

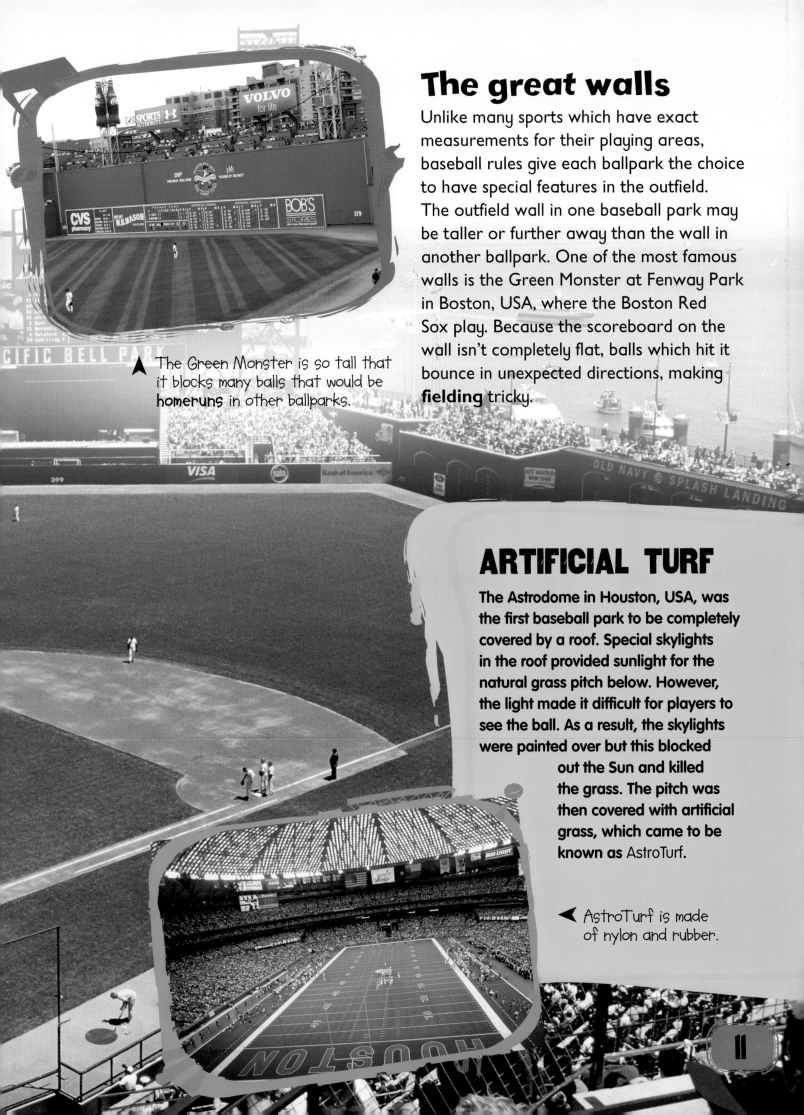

The great walls

Unlike many sports which have exact measurements for their playing areas, baseball rules give each ballpark the choice to have special features in the outfield. The outfield wall in one baseball park may be taller or further away than the wall in another ballpark. One of the most famous walls is the Green Monster at Fenway Park in Boston, USA, where the Boston Red Sox play. Because the scoreboard on the wall isn't completely flat, balls which hit it bounce in unexpected directions, making **fielding** tricky.

▲ The Green Monster is so tall that it blocks many balls that would be **homeruns** in other ballparks.

ARTIFICIAL TURF

The Astrodome in Houston, USA, was the first baseball park to be completely covered by a roof. Special skylights in the roof provided sunlight for the natural grass pitch below. However, the light made it difficult for players to see the ball. As a result, the skylights were painted over but this blocked out the Sun and killed the grass. The pitch was then covered with artificial grass, which came to be known as AstroTurf.

◄ AstroTurf is made of nylon and rubber.

BASKETBALL ARENAS

Most professional basketball games are held in indoor arenas. Many arenas are used for more than one sport, so the surface of the basketball court is made from portable panels of wood that fit together like a jigsaw puzzle. The wood panels are designed to reduce injuries to the players by absorbing some of the force when the players' feet hit the floor. At the same time, the panels are stiff enough to make the ball bounce well.

Locker rooms

Sports players change into their kits in the locker room. After the game, they take showers, get routine medical treatments and meet with reporters in this area. Some locker rooms even have a players' lounge with televisions, video games, stereos and computers to help the players relax before the game.

This modern ➤ locker room is used by the Miami Heat basketball team.

OFFENSE   DEFENSE

MAKING MUSIC

Indoor arenas are often used for concerts and shows, as well as for sporting events. For concerts, workers remove or cover the sport's playing surface to protect it. Then the stage and extra seats are installed. Lights and speakers are hung from the ceiling and placed around the sides of the stage. The centre scoreboard is raised to give the audience a clear view of the stage. For some special events, such as a circus, safety equipment is also installed.

Thousands of fans packed into the Millennium Stadium in Cardiff to watch the singer Madonna in concert. The stadium is usually used for a variety of sports. ▶

▼ Most basketball arenas are shaped like circles. This is the Staples Center, home of the LA Lakers team, in Los Angeles, USA.

MULTI-PURPOSE STADIUMS

Many stadiums are built to be used for more than one sport. A team may play only forty or fifty games in its stadium during the year. That leaves more than three hundred days when the stadium is not being used. For this reason, sports such as ice hockey and basketball often share the same arena. Some football stadiums are also designed so that an athletics track can be installed for special events such as the Olympics.

▲ The Rod Laver Arena hosts the Australian Open tennis tournament, but basketball games, motocross events and concerts are also held here.

Making changes

The Sapporo Dome in Japan is a **domed** stadium that can convert from a baseball park into a football stadium in just a few hours. First, the baseball field's artificial turf is rolled up and stored. Then, a wall opens and a natural grass football pitch moves into the building, hovering on a pillow of air. To make sure the football spectators get the best view possible, the field and several banks of seats rotate until they join up with the other seats in the stadium.

▲ The grass pitch at the Sapporo Dome is kept outside when not in use for a football match.

PLAY BALL

For many years, American cities with both a baseball team and an American football team tried to save money by building one stadium that could be used for both sports. However these stadiums didn't work perfectly for either game. American football fans were too far from the field, while many of the seats for the baseball games weren't even pointing the right way! Soon, teams started building separate stadiums for each sport, often right next to each other.

▲ Monster Park is home to the San Francisco 49ers, an American football team. It used to host the games of the San Francisco Giants baseball team, too.

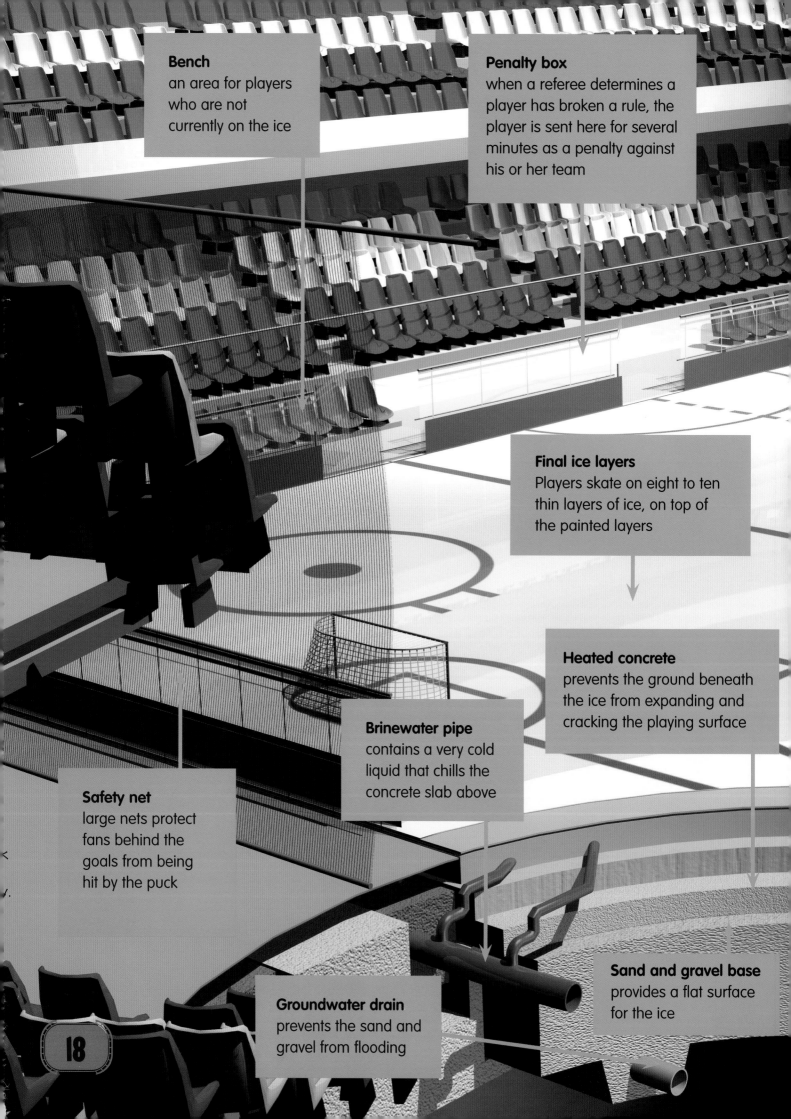

Bench
an area for players who are not currently on the ice

Penalty box
when a referee determines a player has broken a rule, the player is sent here for several minutes as a penalty against his or her team

Final ice layers
Players skate on eight to ten thin layers of ice, on top of the painted layers

Heated concrete
prevents the ground beneath the ice from expanding and cracking the playing surface

Brinewater pipe
contains a very cold liquid that chills the concrete slab above

Safety net
large nets protect fans behind the goals from being hit by the puck

Sand and gravel base
provides a flat surface for the ice

Groundwater drain
prevents the sand and gravel from flooding

Cooling the ice

The ice on a skating rink is only about 2.5cm thick. Below the ice is a flat slab of concrete that is chilled by liquid-filled pipes to keep the ice frozen. The liquid is a type of **antifreeze**, called brinewater, that can be cooled to below 0°C without freezing. Below the pipes is a layer of **insulation** and then a heated slab of concrete. This is because when things freeze, they expand. If the ground beneath the pipes was allowed to freeze, it could damage the playing surface above, so the heated concrete keeps the sand and gravel base of the ice rink warm.

Many markings

The red line in the middle of the rink is called the centre line and divides the playing surface in half. Two blue lines divide the ice into three areas, called zones. There are also nine red spots marked on the ice, called faceoff spots.

▲ At a faceoff spot, the referee drops the puc between two opposing players to restart pla

ICE HOCKEY ARENAS

An ice hockey rink is designed to be as safe as possible for both players and fans. A wall around the edge of the ice keeps the **puck** and players inside the rink. The wall has wooden boards on the bottom, and a clear layer of plastic or extra-thick **safety glass** on the top. There are doors in the boards which let the players onto the ice. The doors open out from the ice so that they do not accidentally catch a fast-moving player. The safety glass and a net that hangs behind each goal allow fans to watch the action while being protected from flying pucks.

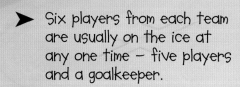

➤ Six players from each team are usually on the ice at any one time — five players and a goalkeeper.

THE PERFECT TEMPERATURE

The freezing point of water is 0°C but ice hockey players like their ice a little colder so that it will let them skate faster. A typical ice hockey surface is kept around -4°C. Figure skaters prefer their ice to be a few degrees warmer so that their skate blades grip the ice better for delicate moves.

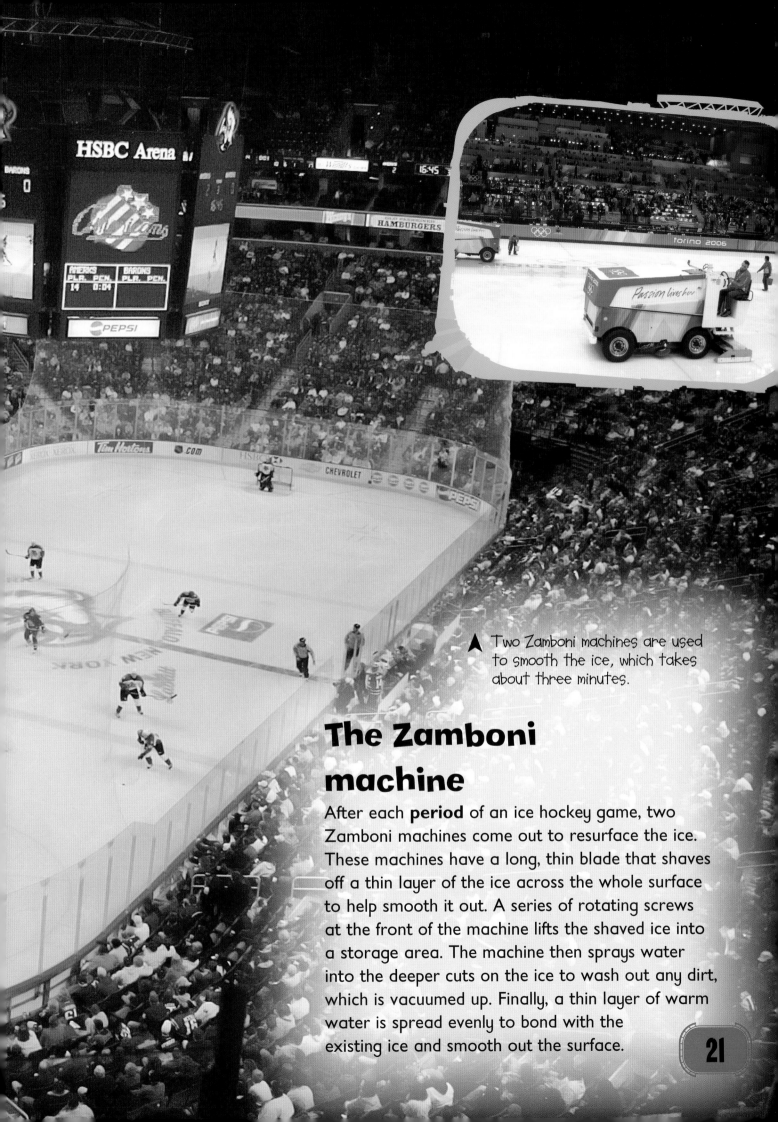

▲ Two Zamboni machines are used to smooth the ice, which takes about three minutes.

The Zamboni machine

After each **period** of an ice hockey game, two Zamboni machines come out to resurface the ice. These machines have a long, thin blade that shaves off a thin layer of the ice across the whole surface to help smooth it out. A series of rotating screws at the front of the machine lifts the shaved ice into a storage area. The machine then sprays water into the deeper cuts on the ice to wash out any dirt, which is vacuumed up. Finally, a thin layer of warm water is spread evenly to bond with the existing ice and smooth out the surface.

The glass
a clear wall above the boards made of plastic or safety glass

Covering the ice

Ice hockey teams and basketball teams often use the same arenas within hours of each other. **Conversion teams** must learn to take the hockey rink apart and quickly build a basketball court. First, workers move all of the glass from the hockey rink into storage. Then, they cover the ice with insulating boards that keep the cold below the surface. Finally, the wooden basketball court is fitted together like a jigsaw puzzle and the basketball goals are put into place. It takes six to eight hours in total.

Different sizes

Ice hockey rinks around the world are all basically the same shape and have the same types of coloured lines painted on them. However, hockey rinks in North America are a little different to rinks in other parts of the world. While international ice hockey rinks are 61 metres long and 30 metres wide, the rinks used in North America's National Hockey League are only 26 metres wide. The distances from one end of the ice rink to the red goal lines and the blue zone lines are also a few metres different in the two types of rinks.

➤ This ice hockey rink is in Edmonton, in Alberta, Canada.

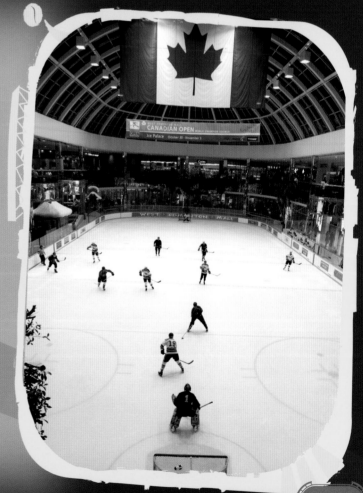

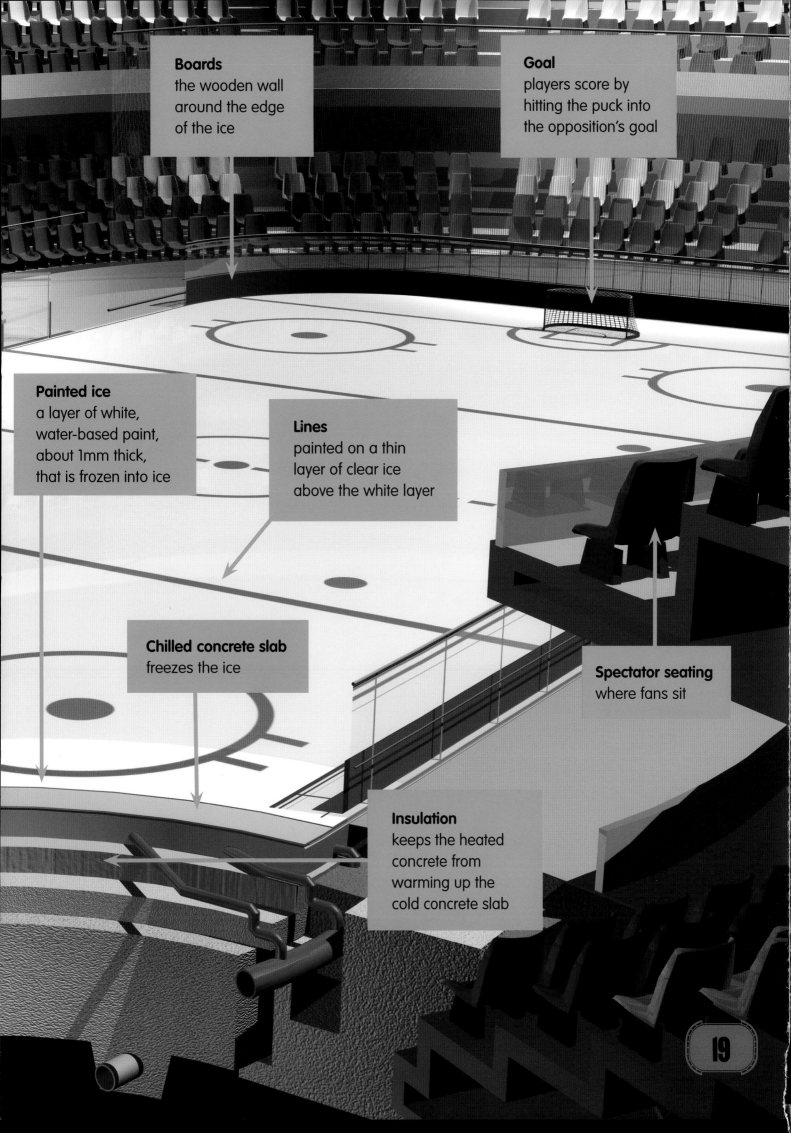

Boards
the wooden wall around the edge of the ice

Goal
players score by hitting the puck into the opposition's goal

Painted ice
a layer of white, water-based paint, about 1mm thick, that is frozen into ice

Lines
painted on a thin layer of clear ice above the white layer

Chilled concrete slab
freezes the ice

Spectator seating
where fans sit

Insulation
keeps the heated concrete from warming up the cold concrete slab

TENNIS STADIUMS

The playing surface of a tennis stadium can be made from grass, clay or hard surfaces, such as cement or plastic. The famous Wimbledon tennis championships are played on a grass surface. The grounds staff work hard to keep the grass in good condition because any small **defect** on the court, such as a bump, can change the way the ball bounces. Clay courts, such as those at the Roland Garros stadium in Paris, are made from crushed brick. This surface slows the ball down more than grass or hard courts.

Meet the media

When covering a sporting event, television and newspaper reporters watch the action from the **press box**, which is usually in the upper half of the stadium. The press box has rows of desks facing a large window overlooking the centre court. For big events or competitions, a separate press room will have small televisions for each reporter, as well as a computer so they can check information quickly.

▼ The main match of the French Open Tennis Championship is played at the huge square court at the Roland Garros stadium.

Groundsmen at the US Open tennis ▲ championships use giant **squeegees** to clear water off the courts.

RAIN, RAIN, GO AWAY

A rain delay during a tennis tournament may last even longer if the court surface is not protected from the water. Extra moisture affects how high the ball bounces and can make the court so slippery that it becomes dangerous for the players. When the rain starts to fall, ground staff will pull out a special waterproof cover to keep the court surface dry.

MOTOR RACING RACING TRACKS

Some of the largest seating areas in the world can be seen at motor racing tracks. These **grandstands** are usually found around the finish line of the race, but may also curve around other parts of the track. Giant television screens allow fans to watch the race even when the cars are on distant parts of the track. A motor racing track, or circuit, can be oval-shaped but usually has lots of curves to make it more challenging for the drivers.

On the track

Motor racing tracks are usually made of **asphalt** or concrete, like any normal road or motorway. However, racing cars use special tyres that are made of softer rubber than ordinary car tyres. These tyres release **resins** that help the car to grip the track better. The turns at an oval circuit are sometimes **banked** to help the cars stay on the road when they go around curves, too.

FACT!

The largest stadium in the world is the Indianapolis Speedway, a motor racing track in the United States that can hold 250 000 spectators.

◄ The Silverstone Grand Prix racing track has many tight curves and bends.

SAFETY FEATURES

Seating areas at motor racing tracks are raised higher above the ground than at other sporting stadiums. This gives spectators a better view and keeps them safe. Concrete walls and strong wire fences also protect the fans from any debris that might fly about if the cars crash.

◄ A concrete wall protects spectators during a high-speed crash.

VELODROMES

A velodrome is an oval-shaped racetrack with banked turns that is used for bicycle races. When cyclists make a sharp turn at fast speeds, they are pulled to the outside of the track by **centrifugal force**. Banked turns help push back against this force, making the bicycles easier to control. Indoor cycle tracks are made from wood, while outdoor tracks may have concrete or asphalt surfaces instead.

▲ Riders warm up and wait for their races in the centre of the velodrome track.

The older, the better

Other sports are always finding new and better surfaces on which to play and race, but the older an indoor cycle track, the better. As the wood in a velodrome track becomes harder and smoother with use, the track often becomes faster. Some new velodromes have even installed an old wooden track from another location instead of building a new one.

FACT!

A velodrome's round track is usually 250 metres long and 7 to 7.5 metres wide.

▼ The coloured lines are a guide for the riders as they race around the track.

STAY IN THE LINES

Velodrome tracks have standard markings painted on them. The area below the red line is the shortest way around the track. Riders must pass anyone in this area on the outside, rather than trying to squeeze past them on the inside of the oval.

AQUATICS CENTRES

Aquatics centres hold swimming competitions such as racing, diving, **water polo** and **synchronized swimming**. Racing events take place in a rectangular swimming pool that is about 1.35 to 2 metres deep. The much deeper **utility pool** is used for diving, water polo and synchronized swimming. Many countries have open air pools which can be covered when the weather is bad.

➤ Aquatics centres have special pools for swimming and diving competitions. This is the Olympic swimming pool in Montreal, Canada.

FACT!

The National Swimming Centre in Beijing, China, is called the Water Cube because its outer wall of **fibreglass fabric** was designed to look like water bubbles. This surface also allows sunlight to shine through and help heat the pools.

Competition pools

An Olympic-sized pool is 50 metres long, although some have moveable walls for shorter races. The lanes are divided by eight, coloured lane ropes that are tied to each end of the pool and float on the surface of the water. Each racing lane has a **starting block** at one end. Most competition swimming pools are heated to keep the temperature between 25 and 28°C.

➤ Starting blocks are slightly raised platforms from which the swimmers dive at the start of the race.

DIVE RIGHT IN!

Competitive divers jump from a diving tower or springboards into the very deep utility pool. They use different boards depending on the type of dive they are going to perform. The diving tower features several platforms at different heights that do not move. Springboards bounce up and down to give the diver more lift when jumping into the dive. Some utility pools have a viewing window underwater, so judges can see how cleanly the divers enter the water.

▲ A diving tower has diving boards and platforms at different heights for practice and competition.

29

RADICAL ROOFS

Many new stadiums are being built with retractable roofs that can be opened on days when the weather is good and closed when it is too hot, cold, windy or rainy. These special roofs also allow grass to grow inside the stadium. The Chase Field ballpark in Arizona, USA, has a roof that can open in just five minutes. Each half of the Chase Field roof has its own motor, so that the roof can be closed halfway if necessary to reduce glare from the Sun.

▼ The two halves of the retractable roof at Chase Field can be operated separately.

FACT!

The largest multi-purpose stadium cover in the world is a tent-like roof with 24 peaks at the King Fahd International Stadium in Riyadh, Saudi Arabia.

Air-supported roofs

Several stadiums around the world have air-supported domed roofs made from layers of fabric that are stronger than steel. High-powered fans increase the **air pressure** inside the stadium, which keeps the roof inflated like a balloon. To keep snow from deflating the roof with its weight, heated air is pumped between the layers of the fabric during a snowstorm. The snow melts and the water runs off.

Some stadium roofs, such as the one on the Tokyo Dome, are made from strong fabric that is held up by air pressure. The Toyko Dome is the home of the Yomiuri Giants baseball team, in Japan. ▶

CABLE-SUPPORTED ROOFS

The Georgia Dome in Georgia, USA, has the largest cable-supported fabric roof in the world. The fabric is held up by a group of cables that form strong triangle shapes, similar to a giant spider's web.

▲ The Georgia Dome is the home of the Atlanta Falcons, of America's National Football League.

SURPRISING STADIUMS

Many of today's stadiums are built not only to provide good views of sporting events, but to get noticed, too. The Allianz Arena in Munich, Germany, was one of the most distinctive used to host games during the 2006 FIFA World Cup. The outside of the building is covered with an inflatable fabric that glows with light. Two different football teams share the stadium as their home pitch. The lights change to match the official colours of whichever team is playing a home game.

▲ There are 4250 individual lights in the outer walls of the Allianz Arena.

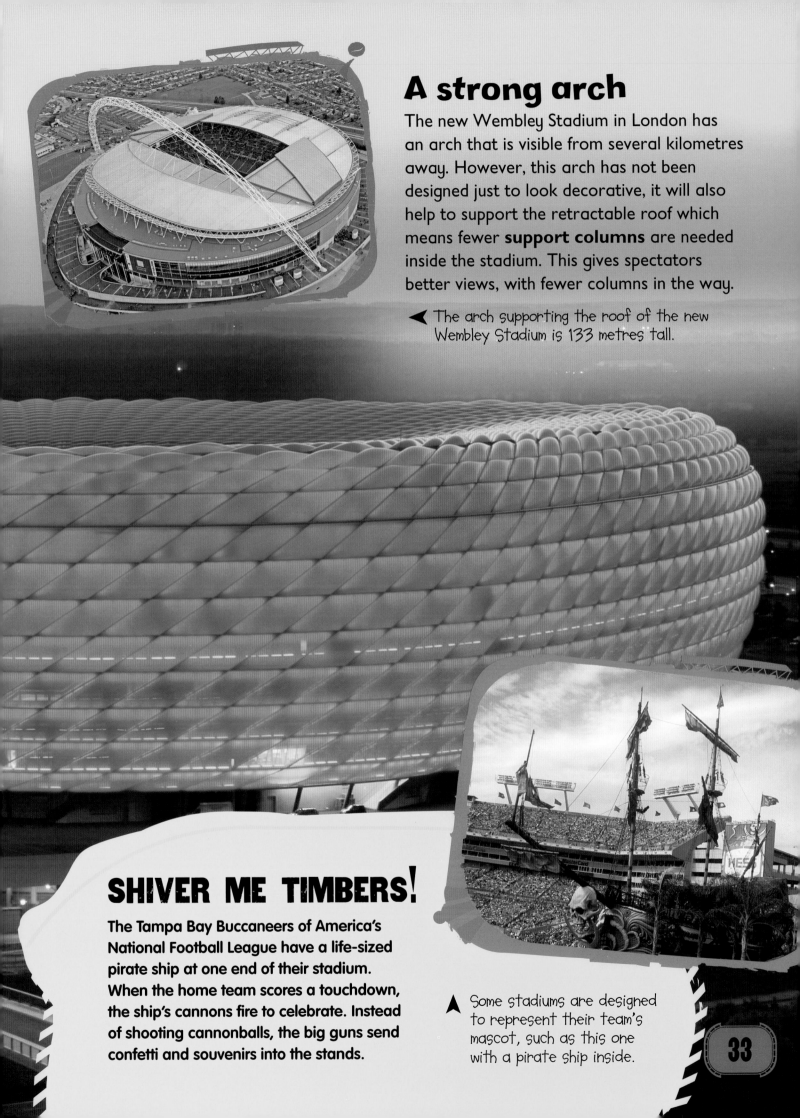

A strong arch

The new Wembley Stadium in London has an arch that is visible from several kilometres away. However, this arch has not been designed just to look decorative, it will also help to support the retractable roof which means fewer **support columns** are needed inside the stadium. This gives spectators better views, with fewer columns in the way.

◄ The arch supporting the roof of the new Wembley Stadium is 133 metres tall.

SHIVER ME TIMBERS!

The Tampa Bay Buccaneers of America's National Football League have a life-sized pirate ship at one end of their stadium. When the home team scores a touchdown, the ship's cannons fire to celebrate. Instead of shooting cannonballs, the big guns send confetti and souvenirs into the stands.

▲ Some stadiums are designed to represent their team's mascot, such as this one with a pirate ship inside.

GLOSSARY

air pressure   The force of air pushing on things.

antifreeze   Something that lowers the freezing point of a liquid to keep it from freezing.

arena   An indoor building in which sporting events are held.

artificial turf   A man-made playing surface that looks like grass.

asphalt   A road surface made from gravel or sand mixed with a sticky, black, tar-like substance.

AstroTurf   A brand of artificial turf, first used at the Astrodome in Houston, USA.

ballpark   A stadium in which baseball games are played.

banked   Sloped.

centrifugal force   A force that acts on objects that are moving in a circle, causing them to move outwards.

conversion teams   People who work to make a stadium that is being used for one sport ready for a different sport.

defect   A flaw.

domed   Covered by a rounded roof.

drainage system   A set of pipes that removes water from the ground.

editors   People who prepare video film for viewing and decide what to show.

fertilize   To add a chemical or natural material to make soil healthier for growing plants.

fibreglass fabric   A material made from very thin threads of glass.

field events   Athletics events that take place on an open grassy area.

fielding   Trying to catch the ball during a baseball game.

figure skaters   Athletes who skate on the ice while performing jumps, spins and dance movements set to music.

foul balls   Balls that are hit by the batter and move outside the foul lines that mark the field of play.

grandstands   A group of seats where people watch a sporting event, especially a motor race.

grounds staff   A group of workers who keep a playing field in good condition.

high-definition video boards   Video screens which have a sharper image and a wider shape than a normal screen.

home plate   A flat piece of rubber which a base runner must touch to score a run, or point, in baseball.

homerun   A hit in baseball which allows the batter to run around all four bases and score a run.

hurdles   An athletics event in which runners race around a track and jump over fences, called hurdles.

infield   The area inside an athletics track or inside the diamond shape on a baseball field.

instant replay   A short video that shows an important moment from a sporting event just after it has happened.

insulation   A material that helps prevent the movement of heat from one surface or place to another.

lanes   The narrow courses on a running track or in a swimming pool, with one lane given to each competitor.

outfield   The area of a baseball field beyond the diamond shape formed by the four bases.

34

period One of three timed sections of play in an ice hockey game.

pitcher's mound A raised pile of earth on which the pitcher stands to throw the ball during a baseball game.

press box An area where reporters work during a sporting event.

puck A hard rubber disk that players try to hit into the goal to score in ice hockey.

relay races Running or swimming races in which several team members take turns completing parts of the course.

resins A sticky substance used to make plastics that helps a car tyre grip the road better.

retractable roof A roof that opens by being pulled back.

retractable seats A group of seats that can be moved or pulled back.

safety glass A type of glass that does not break or shatter easily.

spectator A person who watches a sporting event.

sprinting Running for a short distance at top speed.

squeegees Tools with rubber blades that are used to sweep water from a hard surface.

stadium A large structure or building used for sporting events.

starting block The small platform from which swimmers begin a race.

support columns A tall vertical pillar that helps hold up a building.

synchronized swimming A swimming event in which more than one person moves through the water in unison.

tiers sections of seats arranged above one another, in steps.

traction The grip of something moving on a surface.

utility pool A deep pool used for diving, synchronized swimming and water polo.

video board A very large screen that shows televised images during sporting events.

water polo A sport played in a deep swimming pool in which players from two opposing teams try to move a ball into the other team's goal.

FIND OUT MORE

Find information and photographs of stadiums around the world:
http://www.worldstadiums.com

Discover more about world stadiums:
http://worldstadia.com

Learn more about the Georgia Dome's roof and other stadium domes:
http://www.pbs.org/wgbh/buildingbig/wonder/structure/georgia.html

Watch the Sapporo Dome's hovering football stage:
http://www.sapporo-dome.co.jp/foreign/main_english.html

Find out about new stadiums that are being built:
http://www.sportsvenue-technology.com/projects/

INDEX